Praise for
Who Wants to be a Millionaire
by Judi Deatherage

"*Who Wants To Be A Millionaire* should be required reading for every high school and college student in America. . . . Judi Deatherage has her pulse on the business savvy needs of young people. Her advice on financial matters will make a huge difference in the quality of life for students who read and act on it. . . . The best $10 I have ever spent. This book can change a life from poverty to wealth."

– Gary Griesser, Associate Commissioner
Kentucky Department of Education

"Ms. Deatherage was always able to explain things in a manner that made sense to teens. She made you want to learn more."

– Suzy Smith, former student, Development Manager
Resource Interactive

"This book speaks to people on a basic level. Even adults can benefit from the message."

– Randy Travis, Indianapolis, Indiana

Who Wants to be a

MILLIONAIRE?

A PRACTICAL FINANCIAL GUIDE FOR YOUNG ADULTS

Judi Deatherage

The Clark Group
Lexington, Kentucky

Who Wants to be a Millionaire?

Order for Classroom Use

25 Copies—$200.00 plus s/h
(Equivalent to $8.00 per copy)

Single copies—$9.99 plus s/h

Send orders to:
The Clark Group | PO Box 34102 | Lexington, KY 40588
859 233 7623 | 800 944 3995 | www.KyAlmanac.com

All orders must be accompanied by a check in U.S. funds.
Postage/Handling is 10% of subtotal – $7 minimum, $25 maximum
All sales are final—no consignment orders.

To my husband, H.B.,
for his untiring devotion in giving back to his community.

God has blessed me with a loving husband and family and wonderful friends who have been so supportive. My husband, H.B., has taught me what it means to give time and effort back to his school and community. My first-born, Khristie, has such a special place in my heart. To my twins, Jon and Mike, and their wives, Angie and Cindy, for being the parents of my precious grandchildren, Brayden, McKenzie, Corbin, and Jeffrey. To my brother, Jack Ely, who has replaced my late father as my mentor and the person I always call with financial questions. My sister Joy Sharp and I have shared many special moments, especially as adults caring for our mother, and I love her dearly.

A special thanks to my minister and friend, John Russell, who reminds us that all we possess belongs to God, anyway. To Hugh Wicks and my Lakeside Christian Church choir buddies for the music in my life. To all my friends and colleagues at Boone County High School, but especially those who have allowed me to be their "unofficial financial advisor" and to talk to their students about money: Elaine Feder, Pam Hirn, Jeff VonHandorf, Rick Thompson, Kathie Richie, (and Marilyn Barrett, Ruth Davis, and Ann Loftis at Ryle High School) and to math teachers Bonnie Kroth and Debbie Stidham for the compounding formula. To my friends at Curves who keep me in shape! To George Ridings for answering my questions about insurance and Carlyle Ackley and Jerry Bailer, CPAs, for the most recent tax information. To Barbara and Keith Stuart for believing in me. And I am forever indebted to my dear friends Susan Russell and Ann Eickhoff for their love and encouragement in every area of my life.

Last, but certainly not least, I am so grateful to my former students throughout my teaching career who have had a real passion for learning. I love you all.

Judideatherage@aol.com

CONTENTS

Who Wants to be a

MILLIONAIRE?

INTRODUCTION

AFTER YEARS OF HEARING: "WHY HASN'T SOMEONE TOLD US ABOUT THIS?" I'm determined to get the word out to teens and young adults. I have talked to hundreds of high school students about early financial planning, and their reaction is always the same. They are amazed at the difference it makes if they start an investment program as young adults instead of waiting until they are in their forties or fifties.

My mission is to educate as many young adults as possible about starting at an early age with a savings and investment plan that will carry you throughout adulthood. Our high schools and colleges are not teaching you about one of the most essential elements of adulthood—how to manage your money. You are educated in English, science, math, social studies, business, arts and humanities; all of which are vitally necessary for your world; but the subject of finance is noticeably absent in the curriculum of most high schools and colleges—unless accounting or finance is your major.

Many parents are doing an excellent job educating their children about finances. They may have made sound financial decisions and never had to worry about having enough for their needs. Others may just be getting by and living from paycheck to paycheck.

Parents may avoid the subject of money altogether, finding it just as difficult to talk about money as drugs or sex. They often think you're just not "ready." Many parents don't realize that sharing their mistakes may help you avoid making the same errors. Thus, you do not get any training whatsoever in this vital area of your lives.

This book is written for you, the teenager or young adult, not your parents. I'm sure your parents want the very best for you, but perhaps aren't fully equipped to deal with every area of life. I know that you will be responsible if you are given the right information. It doesn't matter where your parents are financially, whether they've made wise decisions or not—you can be accountable for yourself.

This is an easy-to-read, easy-to-follow plan of action for young adults. While definitely not all-inclusive, it is meant to give you plenty of information to begin your lifetime financial plan and start you on your way to becoming a millionaire. Much of the information included may be completely new to you, but some may be familiar. Use it as a reference book as you emerge into adulthood.

I tell my high school accounting and finance students that nothing would make me happier than to hear that they are, indeed, millionaires because they began financial planning at an early age. I wish the same for each of you who take the time to read this book. I want you to be a millionaire! Please keep reading.

TIME IS ON YOUR SIDE—THE "WOW" FACTOR

WHERE DO *YOU* WANT TO BE IN TWENTY OR THIRTY YEARS? On your way to becoming a millionaire? Or maybe already there? Becoming a millionaire is a matter of *choice*.

It isn't as difficult as you may think. However, a secure financial future doesn't happen overnight. Most millionaires don't get there by inheriting wealth, by winning the lottery, or even by making a hefty salary. They don't always live in prestigious neighborhoods or drive expensive cars. In fact, there may be a millionaire living next door to you right now, even in your unassuming neighborhood.

Attaining prosperity is not a matter of luck, but of careful planning and making good choices. It has nothing to do with how much you *earn*, but everything to do with how much you *keep*. It's simply a choice you make. It's possible—even easy—to accumulate wealth, even with a moderate income. You may not be thinking beyond college and getting your first job, but young adults have a tremendous advantage in this quest for financial independence. That advantage is your youth. **Time** is on your side.

An important concept in long-term investing is "average rate of return." The average rate of return is the annual percentage of interest or growth you earn on your investments over a period of time. Although there is no guaranteed rate, investing over a thirty to thirty-five year period allows the market to fluctuate, and historically it has always recovered from downturns. An average rate of return of ten percent, or possibly more, is not unrealistic for this length of time. Historically, the stock market has averaged 11% over the long term. Let dividends accumulate along with the growth of the stock to compound earnings. We'll talk more about that in Chapter Two.

Although it's never too late to start planning your financial future, teen years are an ideal time to begin investing. The following example shows why it is important to begin saving at an early age.

A nineteen-year-old invests $2,000 a year for ten years in the stock market, then stops and doesn't touch it. At a 10% average rate of return, she will have approximately $1.08 million at age sixty-five, after making a total investment of only $20,000. WOW! But what if she waits until she is twenty-eight and invests $2,000 per year until she is sixty-five—a total of thirty-eight years? At the same average rate of 10%, she will accumulate $728,000, with an investment of $76,000. Still not bad, but check the math. She has invested $56,000 more, and nets a quarter of a million less. To benefit from your investments later in life, start young and stick it out when the market fluctuates. You'll be glad you did!

To comprehend how this happens, you need to understand "compounding." Compounding is earning interest on the interest you have already earned. For example, if you deposit $1,000 at a simple interest rate of five percent, in one year you will have $1,050. The next year, you will earn interest on $1,050 instead of $1,000, or $52.50 instead of $50. The results are amazing when you keep adding to your original amount on a regular basis. The younger you are when you start, the more your money grows. Compounding of interest and dividends over a period of thirty years adds up to financial independence.

For you math wizards, the formula for compounding is $A=P(1+r/n)^{nt}$ where **P** is the original principal, **r** is the annual rate of interest, **t** is the number of years (time), and **n** is the number of times it is compounded in a year. **A**, of course, is the final amount. Remember, this assumes that you are putting all your money into your investment at one time.

The idea is to let your money grow without using it. Although you do need accounts that allow you to use your money for emergencies, this is about long-term savings for financial independence. Retirement is probably the last thing on your mind right now (maybe you haven't even gotten your first "real" job), but early savings will give you options later. Money doesn't buy happiness, but it can provide you with choices.

If you wait until you are forty-five or fifty to think about retirement, it will be very difficult to set aside enough to be comfortable. Less than half of Americans put aside money specifically for retirement. It is estimated that only five percent of people at age sixty-five have more than a million dollars saved for retirement, forty-one percent will still be working out of necessity, and many will be broke! The average American spends eighteen years in retirement (at today's life expectancy). Don't spend those years having to work and wishing you had saved for that period of your life. Beat the retirement clock!

Social Security may or may not be available when you're ready to retire. The current age for benefits for those born after 1960 is sixty-seven, and that age is climbing. You may not be able to collect until you are seventy or older. If you start your career at age twenty-two, you will work approximately forty-five or fifty years before you are eligible for Social Security. Even if Social Security is available, it will not be enough to provide a comfortable retirement. Where do *you* want to be financially?

IMPORTANT INFORMATION

_____

_____

_____

_____

_____

_____

_____

_____

_____

_____

_____

_____

_____

_____

_____

_____

_____

_____

BANKING SERVICES

MOST TEENS ARE FAMILIAR WITH BANKS AND A FEW OF THE SERVICES THEY OFFER. Some of you have a savings account; maybe one started by parents when you were very young. The most common types of bank accounts are "put and take" accounts, or money that is readily available when we need it. Another word for the accounts is "liquid," referring to the ease at which we can convert these assets into cash.

When you get ready to open a checking account, be sure to shop around. Some banks have basic or student accounts with minimal or no service charges if you don't write many checks or have more than three or four ATM withdrawals each month. There may be hefty charges if you go over your limit, so be careful. Some checking accounts pay interest, but usually these accounts require a significant minimum balance, such as $500 to $1,000.

The most important thing to remember about checking accounts is to be sure to keep track of all deposits, payments, and withdrawals in your register. Balance your checkbook every month by comparing your monthly bank statement with your own records so you don't overdraw your account. Your bank will charge $25 or $30 for overdrawing your account, plus you'll pay another $30 or more to the business that took your check. You may also check your balance on-line or through your bank's automated call system.

Automated teller machines, or ATMs, are commonly used to withdraw cash from your account. Your ATM card may allow you to withdraw money from anywhere in the country. But you will probably pay a service charge if you use a machine at a bank other than your own. Those $2 or $4 fees per withdrawal add up quickly. If you are already paying a service charge for your checking account, you could easily rack up $15 to $20 in fees each month. Realize that the balance shown on your ATM receipt is probably not correct if you have outstanding checks, or recently written checks that have not yet been returned to the bank for payment.

You may also have a debit card with your checking or savings account, which allows you to make payments at businesses by swiping your card through a machine at the merchant's counter. The money is taken directly out of your account. The advantage of using a debit card is that you do not have to carry a lot of cash with you. But be sure to deduct expenditures from your check register or savings record. Banks charge an average of $27 on every automatic overdraft. Americans pay $10.3 billion in overdraft charges every year, and debit cards are the main culprits.

Vendors may ask whether you want to use your card as a debit or credit. Money is taken out of your account either way, but charges may be added if you use them as debit cards, even though you may be able to get cash back. You should avoid additional charges if you use them as "credit" cards. Every bank is different; make sure you understand how these cards work at your bank. Experiment with "debit" and "credit" to see if you are charged a fee or ask the merchant if their business charges for the use of these cards. These are not actual credit cards, which you will read about in Chapter Five.

Stay away from "payday" lenders who charge exorbitant (some as high as 300 percent or more) interest rates for cashing a check for you, but not depositing that check until your payday. If you're using these businesses, you're in serious financial trouble.

Banks offer many other services besides checking and savings accounts. Certificates of Deposit (CDs) are accounts that earn a higher rate of interest than regular savings accounts. A set amount is deposited (usually a minimum of $500 to $1,000 or more) and left for a certain length of time, so they cannot be immediately liquidated. For example, you may deposit $1,500 in a CD for one year and the bank guarantees an annual percentage rate for that time period.

In reality, the annual yield is higher than the stated percentage rate because of compounding. Most banks compound daily, which makes your money grow more quickly. Although you may take the money out before the time period is up, you will be penalized with a withdrawal fee. You probably won't receive all your interest, and possibly not all your principal. CDs earn more than regular savings accounts because you agree to leave your money in the bank for a specified time.

Money market accounts, which also pay slightly higher rates of interest than regular savings accounts, are also liquid. However, to get the higher interest rate, you may have to keep a minimum balance of $10,000 or more in your money market. Usually, you may write a specific number of checks per month (sometimes the bank requires that they be for $100 or more) but money markets are a safe place to keep money. It's wise to keep at least three months' basic living expenses in a money market or other liquid account.

The Federal Deposit Insurance Corporation federally insures most banks. Your bank should have a sign indicating it is a member of the FDIC. Each account is currently insured up to $100,000 by this government agency. Make sure your checking, savings, and CDs are covered.

Two other types of organizations offer many of these same banking services. A Savings and Loan Association (sometimes called Thrift and Loans) accepts savings and CD deposits and may provide checking accounts. They earn money to pay your interest by issuing home mortgages.

Another is a credit union, made up of companies or organizations forming their own bank. Credit unions usually pay higher rates of interest on your accounts, and you may also borrow money for car loans or possibly home mortgages at a lower interest rate if you are a member. These organizations may not offer all the services that full-service banks do. Your deposits, however, are federally insured. It is essential to keep some of your money in an insured, no-risk account.

In addition to these common accounts, many banks now have investment departments that offer corporate and government bonds, stocks, and mutual funds, which are discussed in the next chapter.

IMPORTANT INFORMATION

_____

_____

_____

_____

_____

_____

_____

_____

_____

_____

_____

_____

_____

_____

_____

_____

_____

_____

_____

_____

_____

INVESTMENT OPPORTUNITIES

WOULD YOU LIKE TO EARN MONEY FROM MCDONALD'S OR WENDY'S OR PIZZA HUT without ever having to go to work in one of their restaurants? Or from the Gap, Abercrombie and Fitch, or Nike—again without having to go to work every day in their factories or retail stores? That's the idea behind the stock market. Many people avoid buying stocks because they think it's too risky. There is, indeed, a risk in buying stocks. But in the long run, stocks outperform bonds and almost all other types of investments—and without your having to lift a finger (except to dig into your pocket to pay for the stock).

Investments are different from the savings accounts described in Chapter Two. In savings accounts, your principal (the money you have put into the account) doesn't grow but you earn interest on it. Ideally, with an investment, your principal will grow. Savings are federally insured by the FDIC; investments are not. There is no guarantee in investments—no government insurance for the stock market.

When you buy a share of stock, you are actually buying ownership in the company with the right to share in its profits. Most of the large companies you recognize are *public* companies; that is, they sell their stock to the public. Some very well-known companies such as Levi Strauss, LL Bean, Hallmark, and Mars (candy), however, still remain *private* companies—their stock is not sold to the public.

Owning stock is a long-term proposition—we're talking twenty to thirty years. You won't get rich overnight. When you buy stock in a company, you can follow its progress in the financial pages of your newspaper. But don't get excited and immediately decide to sell if you see that it goes down in value.

Because you are young, you can ride out fluctuations in the market. We have recovered from the downturn after September 11, 2001. Traditionally, the market has *always* recovered from downturns and recessions—even from the Great Depression—and has earned an average of 11% over *any* 25-year period. Historically, expansions have lasted a lot longer than recessions.

There are two reasons to buy stock. The main reason is growth—increase in the value of the stock. If you pay $50 for a share of stock today, hopefully over a period of years the value of that stock will go up and you can sell it for more than the $50 you paid for it; maybe quite a bit more.

The other reason is that companies sometimes share the profits they make with their shareholders through dividends issued quarterly, semi-annually, or annually. That's right! They give you part of their earnings just for being an owner of their company. And again, you don't have to go to work for them every day.

Your stock may also become more valuable through stock splits. For example, if you own 25 shares of stock and the company splits shares, you may now own 50 shares. In other words, you own more shares than you originally purchased without having to buy more. Even though your individual shares will be worth less per share, hopefully they will go up in value and you will profit from a stock split. Stock splits are usually a sign that the company is growing.

Remember, we're talking long-term here. You may have heard about people getting rich overnight by buying and selling stocks on the Internet, but that is extremely rare and **very** risky, even if you're an expert. Buy stocks and keep them for many years, reinvesting the dividends to buy more stock. Instead of collecting the $1.00 or $1.50 dividend per share that your company issues twice a year, leave it in your account and let it add to the value of your investment. There may be times when you *should* sell. Generally, though, your policy should be to "buy and hold."

You will need to do some research and investigate companies before buying their stock. Don't buy stocks blindly; examine companies whose products and services you and your friends use. Study established companies that have been around a long time and have a history of profits. "Blue Chip" stocks are the most consistently profitable companies, getting their name from the blue chips in poker, which are the most valuable.

Because there is a greater risk in buying individual stocks, you may want to consider investing in mutual funds. You can buy shares (or fractions of shares) in as many as fifty to one hundred companies that are included in the fund. This spreads out your risk; if one or two or ten companies in your fund go bankrupt, you still have ownership of many other companies.

Spreading out your risk is called *diversification*. Professionals who study the market manage these funds. They know what is going on with the companies in their fund and can make better decisions about them than the average investor. This may be a better way to get started in the stock market than buying individual stocks. You may be able to start investing in a mutual fund with very little money up front ($250 to $500), adding just $25 to $50 per month with an automatic payroll deduction and be on your way to becoming financially independent.

Mutual funds may be purchased at investment companies, broker-age houses, and investment departments in banks. These funds hold approximately 22% of all publicly traded U. S. stocks. Make sure to do some research and find out what the costs are going to be before you invest.

You can avoid funds that hold stock in cigarette companies, alco-hol, or other businesses (sometimes called "socially responsible" funds) if you don't want to put your money into these companies.

Even if you *could* get a guaranteed rate of 8% (extremely unlikely in today's economy!) the following chart illustrates the difference between a high fixed rate of 8% vs. diversification with varying rates of return over a 25-year period:

INVESTMENT COMPARISON OVER 25 YEARS			
INVESTMENT	$100,000	INVESTMENT	$100,000
		$20,000 becomes worthless	$ 0
		$20,000 earns 0%	$ 20,000
INTEREST @	8%	$20,000 earns 5% avg. return	$ 67,727
		$20,000 earns 10% avg. return	$216,694
		$20,000 earns 15% avg. return	$658,800
TOTAL VALUE	$684,848	TOTAL VALUE	$963,221

*Although three out of the five different investments earned less than 8%, the diversified investments still earned 40% more than the fixed investment because of the 10% and 15% returns.

Bonds, unlike stocks, do not make you an owner of a company. Bonds are actually loans made to companies (corporate bonds) or to towns or cities (municipal bonds) on which you will be paid interest. You receive interest on the bonds each year and when the bond matures (usually ten to twenty years) you are paid back the amount you loaned to them. Buy bonds rated Aaa, Aa1, Aa2, or Aa3. Bonds are less risky than stocks and *may* be tax free, but generally do not pay as well over the long run. U. S. Savings Bonds were popular with your grandparents, but they do not pay a very high return, even though they are risk free.

A great way to begin investing is to set aside a specific amount of money each month to put into your investments. An ideal time to begin investing is when you are working part-time and living at home with your parents without many expenses of your own. You can start a custodial brokerage account with a parent or grandparent before you are 18. When you turn 18, remove your custodian's name from the account.

Let's say you are working part-time at your local McDonald's earning approximately $400 per month. You decide you don't want to flip hamburgers for the rest of your life (you'd rather *own* a portion of the company), so you decide to invest in a mutual fund that includes McDonald's in its fifty companies. You begin saving $100 per month for your financial future.

Notice I am not suggesting that you save every penny you earn—I want you to have fun, too! By regularly contributing the same amount of money each month, you are buying stocks whether the price goes up or down. If prices are high, you will get fewer shares. But when prices are low, you end up with more shares. The disciplined-based approach is called *dollar-cost averaging.*

When you get a full-time job, adjust your contributions accordingly. And *always* set aside more for investing each time you get a raise in salary. A good rule of thumb is to consistently save a minimum of ten percent of your salary, but if you can't start there, then begin with three or five percent and work your way up. It's better to set a percentage rather than a dollar amount; that way when you get a raise, you will be saving more as well as having more to spend! Make it automatic and make it easy. (It's also desirable to *give away* a minimum of ten percent, which we will talk about in Chapter Nine.)

Market fluctuations are discussed on TV in terms of *bull* and *bear* markets. A bull market means prices are rising; a bear market is when stock prices fall 25% or more.

It's a *correction* when they fall 10%. For an easy way to remember which is which, think about how those animals attack. The bull charges with his head up (hopefully, you've never seen a bull coming at *you* this way!) and a bear attacks with his paw downward.

How will you have the discipline to save money each month? One way is to have your paycheck directly deposited to your bank account and have the bank transfer part of it to a savings or investment account. If *direct deposit* isn't available, request your employer to automatically withdraw a specific amount out of each paycheck and deposit it to your investment account. This way, you won't have the opportunity to spend it. You won't miss it, because you never get your hands on it.

Regular investing is more important than the amount of the investment. Get in the habit of saving at an early age. **Pay yourself first.** In other words, don't promise yourself you'll invest what you have "left over" at the end of the month. It won't happen! Paying yourself first is an excellent life-long habit to establish while young.

Evaluate your current lifestyle. To have a secure financial future, you must be willing to give up some things today   Do you spend every cent you earn from your part-time job, or do you always put some money aside for that "rainy day?"

If you always run out of money before your next paycheck, take a look at how your money is being spent. Keep track of every cent you spend for a week or two. You may be amazed at how much money you waste. How many snacks and sodas do you consume daily? How many CDs or video games have you purchased in the last month?

Saving a few dollars a day can really add up over the long run. Just $25 per week gives you over $1300 a year to invest. Use what you've been spending for frivolous items to begin your investment plan. You don't need a lot of money to accumulate wealth, just dedication. Investing just $500 per year will reap big dividends if left to accumulate forty-five years. That's only $10 per week. What does it take to save $10 per week? Eliminate one fast-food stop or cut down on snacks and put that money to better use, possibly improving your waistline in the process!

If you're wondering where to put all this money, please read on. Chapter Four just may be the most important chapter in this book.

RETIREMENT PLANNING—YEAR 2045?

THIS COULD BE THE MOST IMPORTANT CHAPTER IN THE BOOK—SO PAY ATTENTION! Retirement is probably the last thing on your mind right now, but **now** is exactly the time to start saving for it. By starting in your late teens or early adult years, you can attain financial independence at a younger age, without having to give up half your paycheck.

Will Social Security, established in 1937, be available for you? With more people collecting Social Security and living longer (**today's** 62-year-old retiree is expected to live another 25 years), the system is in trouble. There is no doubt that changes will have to be made. You begin paying into the system the minute you begin working part time, **and your employer matches your contributions penny for penny.**

The age to collect full Social Security benefits is 67 for those born after 1960. This will probably increase over time; you may have to wait until you are 70 or older before you can collect full benefits. Hopefully you will be able to collect when the time comes. Think of it, however, as a **supplement** to what you have invested and saved for yourself, and not the major source of your retirement income. If you begin early and are disciplined in saving, it won't matter as much if Social Security isn't available for you.

In years past, most people thought they would need less money in their retirement years than they did while they were working. To some extent, that kind of thinking has merit. For example, you may no longer be paying the mortgage on your home, the kids' college expenses may be paid (just imagine what it will cost to send **your** children to college) and you may have less transportation and clothing costs than when you were working.

But many people now feel they want to maintain or even increase their level of income as they get older in order to preserve their standard of living. Other expenses may take the place of working expenses. You may want to travel extensively, purchase a vacation home, help your children with living expenses, or fund your grandchildren's education. We all want the same thing—enough money to live on comfortably. But more than 40% of us will not be able to maintain our current standard of living when we retire. A general guideline is to have enough retirement savings to replace 80% of your annual working income.

According to a 2006 AARP study, 31% of workers 40 and older haven't saved *anything* for retirement and 28% of *current* retirees had not saved any money for retirement. Social Security is the major source of income for 50% of all retirees. And the maximum benefit for workers retiring in 2007 is $2,116 per month. Not enough to go traveling around the world or buy that vacation condo in Hawaii!

The older generation is living longer and healthier; traveling and doing things they didn't have time to do when they were younger—*if* they are financially secure. Think about it—how great is living longer if you're living in poverty or back to flipping burgers just to buy groceries? No matter what choices you make to start saving for retirement, the very best decision is to **start now.**

Retirement accounts are generally tax-deferred, which means you can deduct the amount you contribute from your earned income for tax purposes now, but you pay tax on the withdrawals when you retire. For example, if you earn $35,000 and contribute $3,000 to a tax-deferred retirement account, you will only pay tax on $32,000 of current income. If you are in a 35% tax bracket, that's a tax saving of $750.

Of course, $1 million won't be worth in 2045 what it is today because of inflation (the general rise in prices.) In other words, a dollar won't buy as much then as it does now. (It doesn't really buy much now, does it?) But again, ask yourself this question: Would I rather have $1 million or nothing?

There are three retirement accounts I want to emphasize, although there are others worth mentioning:

401(k)s or 403(b)s

If your employer offers you the option of opening a 401(k), this is the very first step you should take when you get a full-time career job. Limits increase periodically, so find out the current maximum. In 2007, it was $15,500. If possible, fund it to the max each year. Deductions are usually taken directly out of your paycheck, so you won't miss the money. Whatever you contribute comes off your current taxable income.

But the best reason to start a 401(k) is that your employer will probably match a portion of your money. **What—free money?** Did you read this correctly? Sound too good to be true? Yes, many employers offer a 401(k) as part of their benefit package. This is in addition to matching your Social Security contributions. If your employer puts in a dollar for every dollar you contribute to a 401(k), that's a direct 100% return on your money. It's hard to beat that kind of return! Take advantage of this opportunity.

In 2005, about a third of eligible employees in one study hadn't joined their company's plan and lost the "free money" that their employers would have contributed as matching funds. Some companies are now enrolling employees automatically in 401(k) plans, even automatically increasing employees' contributions when they get a raise.

The longer you stay at a company, the more you will benefit from your employer's contributions to *your* account. But if you do leave the company, you may leave your 401(k) in the account to keep growing, or you may transfer it to your next employer's 401(k) (called a *rollover*). Make sure you have worked at your company long enough to take all of your 401(k) with you when you change jobs.

You should have some options in directing the funds in your 401(k). Stay away from putting too large a portion into the company's own stock, especially if the matching funds are in company stock. In 2002, Enron Corporation employees collectively lost $1.3 **billion** of their retirement funds when the company collapsed because their 401(k)s were heavily invested in the company's over-inflated stock. Many of their employees had as much as 50 to 90 percent of their retirement funds in Enron stock. Try not to have more than ten percent of your 401(k) in your company's own stock. **Remember:** diversification is a key factor in retirement savings.

Similar to a 401(k) is a 403(b) for public school teachers, some government agencies, and non-profit organizations. Although your employer does not match funds, your deposits are tax-deferred and the limits may be higher.

INDIVIDUAL RETIREMENT ACCOUNT (TRADITIONAL IRAs)

Traditional IRAs, like 401(k)s, provide for retirement through tax-deferred savings that usually can be deducted from your paycheck. However, they are private accounts and there is no contribution from your employer. The maximum amount you may contribute in 2007 is $4,000 per year, increasing to $5,000 in 2008. There are income limitations as well as limits if your employer offers a retirement plan, so do some research.

Once again, you deduct the amount contributed to a Regular IRA from your current taxable income, and pay tax when you withdraw your money in retirement. For both 401(k)s and Regular IRAs, you may not withdraw money until you are at least 59½ years old without paying a ten percent penalty in addition to the regular income taxes on the money you withdraw. With regular IRAs and 401(k)s, you **must** begin withdrawals at age 70½.

ROTH IRA

A Roth IRA is, in my opinion, the logical choice for young adults (I've been encouraging my students to open Roths since they came out in 1998.) In a Roth, you will not deduct your contribution from your current taxable income (if you make $35,000, you pay taxes on $35,000) but the principal you contribute and the interest you earn is totally tax-free—forever! When you take out your money at age 59½ or later, even if you take out *one million dollars* in a lump sum, you will not pay a penny in taxes—an automatic savings of $300,000 or more, depending on your tax bracket. Think of it as a tax-free savings account.

Another advantage of a Roth IRA is that you may withdraw the principal (not the interest you have earned) from the account because you have already paid taxes on that money. Funds may be used for a down payment on a house, education or medical expenses, without paying a penalty or taxes on the withdrawals. Remember, though, when you take money out of the Roth IRA, you are jeopardizing your retirement. In emergencies, however, this is an important advantage over the Regular IRA.

You also are not **required** to begin withdrawals at age 70½, as you are in a traditional IRA. Older people have started Roth IRAs in the hopes of accumulating funds to leave in their estates to their children—totally tax free. Again, there are some income limitations, which you are not likely to exceed at the beginning of your career. Check with an accountant if you're not sure whether you qualify.

My recommendation is definitely a Roth IRA. If you qualify, this should be the first retirement account you open. You can open a Roth even with a part-time job while you're in school. Then add a 401(k) when you get your "career" job.

With both Regular and Roth IRAs, you must have *earned income*, in other words, a job. If you are working part-time, or only in the summers, and earn $3,000, it could all go into a Roth (or Regular) IRA. You must earn at least as much as you put into your IRA each year.

If your grandma gives you money, but you aren't employed, that money can't be put into an IRA. If she gives you money and you *are* employed, it doesn't matter that the money you put in comes from another source, as long as you have earned the amount you deposit in the account.

If you end up being self-employed as an adult, there are other options for retirement savings, such as a Simple IRA, SEP, or KEOUGH account. If your self-employment doesn't generate much income, a simple IRA is, as implied, easy to open. You may set aside the lesser of 100% of net income or $10,000 annually. However, if you have employees working for you, you may have to contribute for them as well. You may also contribute up to $45,000 of your net earnings from self-employment in a SEP (Simplified Employee Pension) IRA account.

A KEOGH account is not as easy to establish and requires more paperwork. Contributions may be larger, but you may not have to contribute for your employees. Ask an investment counselor or tax accountant for information on these types of accounts for the self-employed.

More and more Americans are being encouraged not to depend too heavily on Social Security and to take responsibility for their own retirement. But we still aren't saving nearly enough—too many people who are eligible don't participate in 401(k)s or these other retirement accounts.

Seniors, use some of your graduation money to start a Roth IRA. Another suggestion for students is to ask your parents or grandparents for help getting started with these funds while you are working part-time during your school years. If they are able, ask them to match funds for these accounts. Emphasize that you are saving for your *future*, not just to use the money in a few years to buy a car! Once they understand you are serious about your financial future, you may be surprised at how willing they are to help you.

A mother who worked at Fidelity Investments understood this concept well. She encouraged her son to save $1,000 annually from his part-time earnings when he began working at age 16, and she matched that amount each year for three years. By the time he graduated from high school, he had $6,000 in a Roth IRA. If he doesn't touch it or add to it, with an average rate of return of ten percent and the magic of compounding, he will have well over half a million dollars at age 65, with only $3,000 of his own money!

Don't put it off—get started *NOW*.

"For of all sad words of tongue or pen, the saddest are these: 'It might have been.'"   – John Greenleaf Whittier

BUY NOW—PAY LATER?

WE AMERICANS ARE OBSESSED WITH *STUFF*. Take a look as you travel across the United States—or in your own town. A young man from Zimbabwe attending a local Bible college was amazed at our "garages" that we rent to store stuff we don't even use (and probably never will) while people in his country are starving. We hang on to things we don't need, while in many countries they struggle just to survive. If you have a roof over your head, food to eat, clothes to wear, and $20 in your pocket, you are better off than 75% of the world's population. Two billion people (40% of the world's population) struggle to live on less than $2 per day. By comparison, most Americans are filthy rich!

Why is it, then, that we think we must have the latest CDs, brand name clothes, the newest sports car, and on and on and on? We are bombarded with advertising that convinces us we MUST have these things or we will be out of the loop, not popular or pretty, or we won't be able to get a girl-friend/boyfriend. We feel we *deserve* to pamper ourselves—we work hard for our money. Teenagers alone spend $3.5 billion a year, including $1.9 billion just on clothes! In 2005, more than 11% of teens had their own credit card.

How do we obtain all this *stuff?* If we don't have the cash, no problem. If we don't make enough money to buy everything we want, no problem. Instant gratification rules! Whip out the plastic and charge it! Using credit ALWAYS TIES UP FUTURE INCOME and prevents you from living off wealth instead of income.

Is what you want today worth spending your future income? Credit can be very dangerous, and young people are prime targets for companies that issue credit cards. Credit enables us to spend money we don't have. That "bargain" is not a good deal if you pay minimum payments and interest for the next five years. Credit is great—for the credit card company. A sign of adulthood is the ability to delay pleasure. A $15,000 credit card limit (or even worse, a $15,000 *balance*) does not make you an adult.

In the 1950s, Diner's Club was the first card that could be used in multiple establishments. The 1960s brought the common use of bank cards. By the 1980s, families were hocked to the limit with mortgages, car loans, home equity loans (see Chapter Six), and credit card debt. Credit card companies come right onto college campuses and offer free T-shirts, pizza, or a free coffee mug (WOW!) just to get you to sign up for their credit cards.

Colleges not only allow this, but encourage it because credit card companies pay the colleges big bucks for the privilege—sometimes in the millions. It is becoming more and more common to target even younger teens by getting parents to co-sign or pre-pay for cards. It is estimated that college freshmen receive an average of **eleven** credit card applications per month.

It doesn't matter that you only have a part-time job, or no job at all. They want you as a customer, and they'll do whatever it takes to achieve their goal. If they get you started on their card at a young age, they figure you will be a loyal customer throughout your life. And you very well may be a life-long customer—it may take you a lifetime to pay off what you have charged to your card while in college! Twenty-eight percent of students with credit cards "rollover" debt each month (don't pay the balance in full).

Even a balance of $2,500, at an interest rate of 17%, will take *thirty* years to pay off if you only make a minimum payment of 2% each month, and will cost you $7,700 in interest. A balance of $20,000 paid over a ten-year period at 18% would cost $23,200 in interest alone. If you had invested those monthly payments and *earned* just 7% for those ten years, you would have accumulated $62,674.

The average student loan carried by college grads is above $18,000, and it is becoming more and more common for students to have $5000 or more in credit card debt by the time they graduate. Much of the time the credit cards have been used for clothes, pizza, beer, and entertainment—not for tuition, books, or other college essentials. Is this worth tying up ten to fifteen years of future income? Do you really want to pay for that pizza for the next twenty or thirty years? Make sure you are using student loans and other college funds for college expenses and not for unnecessary clothes, food, or entertainment. You don't want to still be paying off student loans when you're a grandparent! Something else to keep in mind: college debt may force you to go back to living with your parents after you graduate. You may be part of the "boomerang" generation—those that return home after graduation because they can't afford to live on their own.

Credit is an extremely useful tool that you will need as an adult. Our society could not function without it. How many people do you know who could pay cash for a house, or even a car? Credit should be just that—a tool. Not a way of life.

Before you buy anything on credit, assess the true value of what you are buying. The $25 item may cost you more than $50 by the time you finally pay it off. Even if you pay with cash, you are giving up the opportunity to put that money to work for you for the rest of your life. Instead of buying two CDs or two Abercrombie & Fitch shirts, buy one and invest what you would spend on the second item.

Learn to control your spending. Before you make any purchase, think about the cost as opposed to putting that money into your retirement savings. Figure out the cost of credit and add that cost to your purchase. Then decide if the item is really worth it. Avoid the "keeping up with the Joneses" mentality. One study shows an average credit card debt of $4,358 for adults ages 25-34.

There *are* some advantages of using credit cards. They allow you to order on line (be careful not to get carried away with that, too!) and to have the convenience of not carrying a lot of cash with you. One of the most important advantages of using credit is to establish a credit rating, which will definitely benefit you later in life and is one of the most important things over which you have control as an adult. You will need credit to buy a car, a home, or maybe start your own business.

Make sure to record the account numbers of all your cards and the phone numbers to call if your card is lost or stolen. It's a good idea to make a copy of each card you carry. Your liability is limited to $50 per card if your card is lost or stolen. If you carry seven or eight cards, however, that is still a chunk of change.

Three major credit bureaus (Equifax, Experian, and Trans Union) keep track of your credit score. Prospective lenders use it to determine whether they will take a chance and extend credit to you. Even prospective employers may check your credit score as a measure of your character.

The connection between credit scores and job offers can be a problem for unaware students. High student debt may prevent you from landing that perfect job.

Credit card companies want you to continue using their card—they want to keep your business and may lower your rate if you ask—*if* you haven't made late payments or gone over your limit.

Higher scores may mean lower interest rates. It's like having a "good student" discount on car insurance. Good credit scores may also affect the amount of the deposit required to set up your utilities when you're on your own. Even the cost of your cell phone may be cheaper with a high credit score!

The general range of scores is from 300 to 850. Excellent is above 730; good is 700-729. Limited or no credit is extended if your score is below 585. If you pay your bills on time and are not over-extended, you'll score high. Late payments, current balances, and maximum credit are all recorded on your credit report. Know your score. Mid-700 and up will get you the best interest rates.

You may receive a free copy of your credit report once a year by calling Experian (888-397-3742), Equifax (800-685-1111) or Trans Union (800-269-0271). Or go to www.annualcreditreport.com. It's a good idea to get a copy at least every couple of years to be sure your credit is accurate. Report any discrepancies. You also may receive a copy of your report free if you are turned down for a loan.

Most bankruptcies are filed because of overspending on "stuff." Is bankruptcy an option if you are seriously in debt or is it just an easy way out? There are two types of bankruptcies. A Chapter 7 bankruptcy eliminates all debt and stays on your credit report for ten years. Chapter 13 provides a payment plan, waiving interest and penalties and stays on your credit report for seven years. Neither eliminates student loans or unpaid taxes. Is it a cop out? If you make a pledge to repay money, you are obligated to honor that commitment. New laws have made it more difficult to file bankruptcy; only you can decide if bankruptcy is a reasonable way to handle your debt.

If you find yourself owing more than you can pay each month, **STOP USING CREDIT!** Pay off the cards with the highest interest rates first, and use "plastic surgery" (cut up the cards). Close accounts as you pay them off. Then you are not tempted to rack up more debt. Set a "D-Day"—a date when you want to be debt free, or individual dates for each card. Then *stay* out of debt! If your cards are maxed out, or close, it won't help your credit score to just make minimum payments.

Take steps to reduce your expenses. Stick to a budget. Take your lunch to work instead of going out and don't stop for coffee and a Danish every morning before you even get to work (these two things alone could save you up to $50 per week). Eat dinner out less frequently—or not at all for a while. Exercise at home or walk in your neighborhood instead of paying monthly fees at your local health club (although sometimes friends at the gym can be an incentive to keep exercising!) You can't be certain you'll have a job tomorrow, but you can be certain that the bills will still be due. Take control of your money and make sure your expenses are less than your income.

In recent years, identity theft has been a major problem. Be extremely careful of your card numbers, *never* giving them out over the phone to someone calling you. Report fraud immediately to all three credit agencies.

Don't count on future paychecks to pay current debt. When you get a raise, use it to pay off debt. A bigger paycheck can make your financial situation worse if you spend it all—and charge more! You have more control over what you spend than what you make. We feel "entitled" to material things we can't afford; after all, our hard work justifies the **stuff** we buy. Think about it before you make that purchase.

When you turn 18, if you're not there yet, you will be bombarded with credit card offers. *Be selective!* Although you may not be able to get the best rates for your first card, your goal should be a card with no annual fee and the lowest interest rate possible. (Of course, if you always pay in full each month, the interest rate isn't that important!) "Prestige" cards may charge annual fees of up to $50 just to carry their card.

Beware of "teaser rates"—those offers that come in the mail offering extremely low rates that are only good for a few months, or only good if you are transferring balances from other cards. The rate may jump as high as 15% to 18% after those initial months of low rates. There are also additional fees when you transfer balances from one card to another.

If you do use credit cards, make sure you only buy what you can afford to pay for *in full* at the end of each month. When you get your statement, it will show a "minimum payment." If you only make the minimum payment, you will be paying for years on the purchases you make. Be sure to pay the entire balance each month to avoid paying finance or service charges.

Many people (young *and* old) buy what they can't afford, make minimum payments, max their credit card out, then apply for a new one and start all over again. Don't shop around for a new card too long—prolonged inquiries can hurt your credit score. Many families are carrying $6000 to $8000 or more in credit card debt on several cards and never get out of debt. The average is $8,000, including those with no debt at all. Those that have credit card debt are in hock for an average of $12,000.

They are using their future income to pay for the *stuff* they buy now.

More than 800,000 Americans file for personal bankruptcy each year. Bankruptcies filed by young adults under 25 almost doubled from 1991 to 1999 and, in fact, young people in their twenties now have the highest bankruptcy rate in the U. S.

However, if you *never* use credit, you won't establish a credit rating. Limit yourself to one or two cards with low limits, and pay them in full each month. Credit card companies don't want people who pay off their cards each month. They go after the ones who make minimum payments so the credit card companies chalk up the interest. You can request your credit card company to keep your limit low. Refuse to accept raised limits. Using credit is the *opposite* of investing; instead of gaining 8%-10% or more, you're *paying* 10%-18%. Don't tie up your future income by getting in credit card debt.

You *do* have a choice when it comes to credit. You can choose to live either within your means or above your means. Many Americans are choosing the latter and are realizing too late that they have to pay for the extravagance in their earlier years at a time when they should be thinking about retirement. We're only saving half of what we need and spending twice as much as we can afford. Don't be a slave to *stuff* or to your social life. Tell your money where to go instead of wondering where it went.

Begin tracking where your money goes—starting *TODAY*. Financial security has nothing to do with being rich. The real key to financial success is to live on *less* than you earn—a lesson many adults need to learn!

"Better to go to bed supperless than wake up in debt."   – Ben Franklin

IMPORTANT INFORMATION

BUYING A HOME AND OTHER ASSETS

THERE IS A DIFFERENCE BETWEEN *SECURED* DEBT AND *UNSECURED* DEBT. Credit card debt is unsecured—you get to borrow money or buy *stuff* or services by just signing on the dotted line. Cars and houses are *secured* debt—in other words, the bank gets them back if you default on your loan (you forget to make payments). Now "survival debt" is making its way into the American scene. Charging groceries and everything else and carrying a balance on all of it—definitely not a smart way to live.

You may already have purchased your own car. Which car did you choose—the newest model sports car or a late model used car? (Did you check to see how much you would pay for the insurance?) Ninety percent of the world doesn't own a car, yet we may feel deprived if we don't have one of our own at age sixteen.

Cars are **not** investments; they depreciate (decrease in value) as soon as you drive them off the lot. Think carefully about the kind of car you need. Do you drive a lot of miles to school or work? Then look for a car that gets good gas mileage. If you want a car that will impress your friends, figure out the total cost (including loan interest) to see if it's really worth it. It may make much more sense to buy a used car.

Should you finance the car for two, three, four, five years? Some dealers now offer loans for 72 months (six years) to finance a new car. Of course, the longer the time, the more you will pay in interest. But there is another factor to consider. If you finance a car for five or six years, at the end of three years, you will probably owe more than the car is worth. If you are unfortunate enough to have an accident and total your car, the insurance company will only pay the book value. If you owe more than that, you will still have to pay the rest of your loan. It's called being "upside down" on the loan. If you can't make the payments for a three-year loan, chances are you are buying more car than you can afford or need.

Another recent development in car loans is an offer to "eliminate" the amount you owe on your current car in order to buy a new one. Don't be fooled into thinking they are getting rid of your debt! In reality, the dealer is just rolling that amount into the cost of the new car, so your new car already is worth less than the loan you have on it. Don't get caught up in such schemes.

The biggest investment for many families is their home. There are many reasons to buy a house. Financially, it is usually a wise decision. That's because the value of the house (unlike your car) generally goes up over a period of years, while the mortgage (the amount you owe on the loan) goes down. The difference between what you owe on your house and its current market value is called equity.

Depending on where you live, the average cost of a "starter" home (read: *small*) could be well over $100,000. Traditionally, mortgage lenders have required 20% as a down payment on a house. That's a minimum of $20,000 on even a very modest (read: *small*) house. Some young people are fortunate enough to have parents who help them with the down payment or who are willing to lend it to them.

It is possible to borrow more than 80% of the home's value, however. Some loans are available with only 5% down. But with a down payment of less than 20%, you will probably be required to pay Private Mortgage Insurance. PMI was established by lenders to insure payment if you default on your loan. It will add as much as $50 or more to your monthly payment, depending on the amount you borrow. Once PMI is added to your loan, it is very difficult to get rid of. You must pay the loan down to 80% of the home's value and obtain a current appraisal.

Don't buy a house based on two incomes if you plan to be a stay-at-home mom. Try to live on one paycheck (save the other) for six months to one year before having a child or buying a home.

Do a lot of research before buying. Look not only at the house, but the neighborhood, community, schools, churches, businesses and the general area. You may be there a long time. Hopefully, the value of the house will increase, and you will build equity.

A word of caution is necessary here. You may have heard of "Home Equity Loans." These are loans based on the difference between the value of the house and what you owe on your first mortgage. For example, let's say you live in a $150,000 home and you still owe $100,000 on your mortgage. A mortgage company or bank might be willing to lend you 80% or more of the $50,000 equity you have accumulated. Some lenders are even willing to lend you 125% of the value of your house.

A home equity loan may be used for cars, home remodeling, education expenses, travel, entertainment, eating out, clothes, anything. It is used as a line of credit; in other words, you could have up to 125% of the value of your home to spend any way you want. You just use the checkbook they give you and write checks for whatever you desire. You get the idea? It is very easy to spend this money, but you're putting up your house as collateral, which means if you default and can't pay the loan, you'll lose your home.

Home equity loans can be useful tools (just like credit cards) when used carefully. But, like credit cards, many families have gotten into serious financial trouble by overextending themselves with these loans. Home equity loans keep you from building equity in your house and, as a result, your investment suffers.

The current housing market has been in a slump for over a year. Values of some house are declining and the house may be very difficult to sell. Foreclosures are occurring because many people borrowed more than the value of their house or bought a bigger house than they could really afford. Once again, don't let your preoccupation with "stuff" override your common sense.

When you buy a house, you may deduct the mortgage interest from your taxes as an itemized deduction. The same is true of the interest on home equity loans. Interest you pay on credit cards and most other loans is not tax deductible. Because of this home mortgage deduction, young people buying their first home usually start itemizing deductions (even if they haven't in prior years) and end up paying less in taxes.

If you're thinking about buying a condo as a starter home, add the monthly condo fees to the mortgage payment to be sure you can afford your monthly payments. A condo makes sense if you don't want to handle the yard work or be responsible for outside maintenance. But keep in mind there could be additional assessments levied if your homeowners' association needs additional money. Ask to see their records for the past several years.

As you get older and have more money to invest, other opportunities may arise for additional investment assets. Rental property is one area. Real estate, in general, usually increases in value. Apartment buildings, single-family homes, business property, and even vacation homes are types of rental property you may investigate if you find yourself with extra money. Keep in mind, however, that these money-making opportunities also carry risk and there is work involved in keeping the property in good rental condition.

At some point in your life, you may get tired of working for someone else and want to "be your own boss." You may decide to start your own business. There are many opportunities out there, but there can also be big risks involved. A large number of businesses fail within the first five years.

If you decide this is the route you want to take, make sure you know the product or service you are selling and make sure your business plan is realistic. Most new owners find they need another source of income during the first few years of business because their business does not make enough for them to have a salary. New owners are also sometimes surprised at the number of hours they must work. It's definitely not for everyone.

You will need to be in good financial shape for a bank to lend you money for a business venture. They will ask for a net worth statement, which is a financial statement showing your assets and your liabilities (what you owe). The difference is your personal net worth. If your credit is already over-extended, banks will not risk lending you money for a business that may be subject to failure.

One form of business that traditionally has less of a failure rate is a franchise. You're familiar with franchises such as McDonald's, Wendy's,

Pizza Hut, and many others you could name. They are individually owned businesses, but are under the control of a "parent" company. The parent company helps you get started, provides training for both the retail and the accounting, and offers many other services. These services are not without cost, though. Franchise fees may be as much as 10% of your total sales, and initial start-up costs may be extremely high.

Name recognition is one reason to go with a franchise. But the control of the parent company will prevent you from making some of your own decisions. You are definitely under their power and can only sell the products and services they provide. Again, carefully research your options if you want to be an entrepreneur.

IMPORTANT INFORMATION

_____

_____

_____

_____

_____

_____

_____

_____

_____

_____

_____

_____

_____

_____

_____

_____

_____

_____

_____

_____

_____

INSURANCE—PROTECTION AGAINST LOSS

THERE ARE DOZENS OF TYPES OF INSURANCE TO PRO-TECT YOU AGAINST A MULTITUDE OF RISKS. You can, without doubt, be over insured; but it is more dangerous to be *under* insured.

CAR INSURANCE

If you are of driving age, you're probably familiar with car insurance, so let's start there. If you are under the age of 25, automobile insurance can be very expensive. You should get a better rate if you are included in your parents' policy, or if you leave your car at home while you're away at college. If you purchase a car, research the cost of insurance for the car you want. The sportier the car, the more insurance will cost.

Collision insurance covers damage to your car in an accident. Medical and hospital costs are covered as a result of an accident. Most states require you to have liability insurance on the car you drive to protect those you may injure or whose property you may damage. Comprehensive covers vandalism if someone spray paints or "keys" your car.

If you are driving a clunker, it may not be worth it to buy collision or comprehensive coverage. You may just want to stick with liability coverage if the car is not worth much anyway. The higher your deductible (the amount you pay up front in case of an accident or damage to your car), the lower your premiums will be. The easiest way to lower the cost of insurance is to raise your deductible; for example, from $250 to $500.

HOMEOWNERS' INSURANCE

You will not be able to obtain a mortgage to buy a home unless you have proof of insurance coverage on the house. Make sure you cover the cost of replacing the house (not what you paid for it) and that you also include damage to the contents at the current market value.

RENTERS' INSURANCE

Teens and young people may not be familiar with renter's insurance. Many people (including adults) don't realize that when you rent an apartment, the landlord's insurance just covers the building itself and the "common" areas, such as hallways and stairs. Your individual possessions are not covered for fire in your apartment or for smoke damage from a fire in someone else's apartment.

Even if you start out with "hand-me-down" furniture that no one else wants, you might be surprised at the value of your other belongings. Most young people have stereos, TVs, computers, and other electronic equipment that would be expensive to replace if they were damaged by fire or smoke. Jewelry, clothes, and other household items add to the list. None of these would be replaced by your landlord's fire insurance.

Renter's insurance is inexpensive and is definitely worth the cost. If you are going away to college, your parents' insurance policy may cover you in a dorm room. With today's computers and other electronic equipment that incoming freshmen take with them to school, coverage through your parents' policy or a separate renter's policy is a *must*. It's possible that you may be covered by your parents' policy even if you are living in an apartment off campus. Make sure you have liability coverage. Some policies pay the depreciated value of the lost items while other policies will cover replacement costs. The latter, of course, is better. Check into it!

LIFE INSURANCE

Most young people aren't thinking of death, and rightly so. But once you have a job or a spouse or children (or debt), you need to think about life insurance coverage. This is true for both males and females, especially if both are contributing to the family's income. When you get a full-time career job, your employer may offer low-cost group term life insurance. How much you need, of course, will vary according to your responsibilities. But certainly take advantage of any life insurance an employer offers.

The time to buy life insurance is while you're young. Premiums (what you pay for the policy) are based on age, health, occupation, and hobbies. In other words, if you go mountain climbing every weekend, your premiums will be higher than someone whose hobby is stamp collecting. How much do you need? There's no set amount. Sit down and figure out how much your dependents need to live on if something should happen to you.

There are two basic types of life insurance: term insurance policies and permanent life policies. The *face value*, or *death benefit*, is the amount payable upon your death and is generally non-taxable. You will name one or more *beneficiaries* who will receive the death benefit.

TERM LIFE INSURANCE

Term insurance is the most basic form of life insurance, and the cheapest. It covers you for a specific period of time and offers temporary protection. If your employer provides life insurance, it is usually term insurance. The premium initially is lower than for permanent life insurance, but may increase as you get older. The policy may terminate if you switch jobs, unless your policy has a conversion clause or is guaranteed renewable. Make sure your term policy has both of these features. Term insurance is often used as protection when taking out a loan to insure the debt will be repaid, and is the premise for the PMI insurance mentioned in Chapter 6.

If you are not covered at work, term insurance may be the most affordable type of life insurance, at least initially. If you die within the time stated in your policy, the insurance company will pay your beneficiary the face value, or death benefit, of your policy. Term insurance does not accumulate cash value and usually does not earn dividends. It ends after a certain number of years or at a certain age.

Your premium will probably increase every time you renew. However, you may be able to purchase 5- 10- 20- or 30-year level term insurance, or even level term payable to age 65, which enables you to pay the same amount for premiums over that period of time. Decreasing term allows you to pay the same premiums, but your death benefit decreases each year. This is useful if you are trying to provide funds for your spouse to pay off a home mortgage.

PERMANENT LIFE INSURANCE (CASH VALUE INSURANCE)

When you purchase a permanent life policy, you traditionally pay a fixed premium for as long as you live, or until you quit paying for the policy. The buildup of cash value is the main reason your premiums usually remain fixed for the duration of the policy. The insurance company will pay a predetermined benefit when you die. Permanent life insurance accumulates cash value at a fixed or variable rate of interest, tax deferred, and these policies may also be eligible for dividends. Permanent insurance may also be referred to as "whole life," "universal life," or "variable life" policies.

Permanent life insurance eliminates the problem of future insurability. You will be covered as long as you pay the premiums, no matter what your health status may be. The cash value (dividends and/or interest) may build enough to pay the premiums as you get older, so you will continue to be covered with little or no out-of-pocket premiums.

You cannot simply withdraw the cash value of your policy, even though it is "your" money. You may surrender the policy for its cash value, make a partial withdrawal, or request the cash value as a loan. The death benefit will be reduced permanently by the amount of the withdrawal or temporarily by the outstanding loan balance. The death benefit is restored when the loan is paid in full. The company will charge you interest (at a variable or fixed rate) to borrow against your policy. But loans are generally not taxable and may provide needed cash in an emergency. Insurance companies consider loans an "advance" against the death benefit.

If you do decide to stop paying the premiums and surrender the policy, the cash value is yours. You will pay taxes on that part of the cash value that exceeds your total premiums at the time of surrender. Permanent policies may also have the option of a monthly income (called an annuity) available to you that will supplement your retirement income if you have had the policy for a certain number of years.

Only you will be able to decide whether to buy term or permanent insurance. Keep in mind that the only way to receive anything from term insurance is to die. It has been compared to paying rent—you may rent an apartment for 10 or 15 years, but when you move out, you leave with no equity and nothing to show for your money.

If you decide on term insurance, make sure your policy is guaranteed renewable (you can renew it without a physical exam) and that you have the option of converting it to permanent insurance (usually available within the first several years). Sometimes an affordable option would be a combination of permanent life insurance and an added "rider" of term insurance. An affordable combination, for example, might be $25,000 worth of permanent insurance and a $75,000 term rider that may be converted to permanent insurance later.

WILLS

While you're thinking about life insurance, also think about having a will drawn up. Many people think because they aren't wealthy, they have no need for a will. If you die *in testate* (the legal term for not having a will), your state will decide who gets your property—*and* your children, if they are under 18 years of age. The most important reason to have a will is to name a guardian for your children. This determination should be *yours*; don't leave such an important decision up to the state or the courts.

A trust can be created along with your will to help manage your assets until your children are old enough to handle money wisely. You can declare an age (such as 25) that all your children should reach before dividing your estate among them to prevent the money from being squandered. A trustee is appointed to distribute the funds as needed.

HEALTH INSURANCE

Health insurance is an absolute necessity, and there are many choices. Hopefully, your employer will fund most or all of your health insurance. But with health care costs rising, health insurance premiums have skyrocketed, and the assumption that employers will pay for it may no longer be valid. Many small (and sometimes large) companies simply can no longer afford to pay full health coverage for their employees.

Health Maintenance Plans (HMOs) take care of your health care needs as long as you use their doctors, hospitals, and clinics. Be sure to look over the participating doctors carefully. Your "primary care physician" is your family doctor, but most of the time specialists must be on the list, too. If you are unsure whether the doctors you have been seeing accept your health care choices, ask them.

If you lose your job, you may qualify for a COBRA plan, which will allow you to continue your employer health coverage after you've been laid off or have voluntarily left your job, generally for up to eighteen months. You will have to pay the full premium for this coverage, so it will be costly.

Most plans offer some type of prescription coverage. Many people have no clue what medicines cost. We pay our co-payment of $10, $15, or $20, and complain about the "high cost of medicine." In reality, those prescriptions may be as much as $50 to $150 or more for a 30-day supply. If it is available to you, select a plan with prescription coverage.

DISABILITY INSURANCE

While young adults may think about purchasing life insurance, you don't always realize that you are *five times* more likely to become disabled during your working years than you are likely to die. Disability coverage protects you if you are injured or become ill and cannot work for a period of time. The waiting period may be 30-60 days before coverage begins. If you are not able to work for six months to a year, will your family be able to stay in your house and live comfortably? This insurance may sometimes be purchased through your employer. It's worth looking into.

Don't confuse disability insurance with workman's compensation insurance. Every state requires employers to have workman's compensation insurance in case you are injured on the job. If you are injured elsewhere, or become ill, workman's comp doesn't cover you.

UMBRELLA COVERAGE

No, this does not cover lost umbrellas! In addition to home and auto coverage, lots of families have an "umbrella" policy that covers losses or liability above the limits of your other policies. It is extended personal liability coverage that, combined with all your other policies, usually gives you $1 million more in protection. With the frivolous lawsuits being filed in today's courts, it may even be worth purchasing an additional **$2 million** in umbrella coverage.

OTHER TYPES OF INSURANCE

Dental and vision insurance cover your teeth and eyes. Flood insurance is required if your home is in a designated flood plain. Travel cancellation insurance covers losses if you have to cancel a trip because of illness or death in the family. Flight insurance may be included free if you charge airline tickets on your credit card. Dreaded disease coverage pays if you develop a specific disease such as cancer (don't waste your money— just be sure you have adequate health insurance.) Long-term care insurance pays if you are confined to a nursing home, an assisted-living facility, or need in-home care. (Two out of every five adults over age 65 will need long-term care, but don't even *think* about this until you're in your fifties.) Extended warranties cover your toaster if it breaks. (Again, don't waste your money.) Pet insurance covers veterinary expenses for Fido.

Get the picture? All insurance protects against loss. If you have adequate health insurance, term life insurance and a good homeowner's policy, you shouldn't need much more. You have to draw the line somewhere and choose to protect yourself and your family against only the events that are most likely to happen. Once again, do your homework!

IMPORTANT INFORMATION

IMPORTANT INFORMATION

_____

_____

_____

_____

_____

_____

_____

_____

_____

_____

_____

_____

_____

_____

_____

_____

_____

_____

_____

GET INTERESTED AND GET EDUCATED

DON'T UNDERESTIMATE THE VALUE OF AN EDUCA-TION. There are many ways to be educated besides formal schooling. One advantage of a college education, though, is that it enables you to be a well-rounded individual. It gives you an opportunity to choose from many areas of interest, as well as meeting people not only from all over your state but, in many cases, the entire world.

The financial rewards of a college degree are compelling. The typical college graduate will earn approximately $20,000 more per year than a high school graduate. You do the math—that may be a million dollars difference if you work for 40-45 years. Of course, the higher your degree the more your earnings *should* be. These, of course, are average figures. We can all come up with exceptions, especially when you think of sports stars and other high-profile occupations.

If your parents are able and willing to provide a college education for you, by all means take advantage of this opportunity. Maybe you can't wait to get away to school and be on your own, away from your family. If your parents are funding your education and you graduate without a ton of debt graduating with you, ***thank them!*** They've probably made great sacrifices in their own lives to be able to send you to school.

The value of education is measured in terms of the benefit to the student as well as the cost. Free seminars may be more valuable to you than taking an expensive course at your local university. Take advantage of opportunities that don't cost a lot. Consider working part-time for a company that will reimburse you for the classes you take.

The cost of a college education has skyrocketed in the last few years—the four-year average, even at a state school, is anywhere between $30,000 and $75,000. Private colleges are much more. Of course, you can save money by living at home or attending a community college for a couple of years before transferring to a university to get your degree.

It's possible to find grants and scholarships to help fund your education. Many scholarships go unused because no one has applied for them. Some of my own students that qualified for scholarships didn't apply because they just didn't want to write the essay or fill out the application. Talk to your school counselor and *be persistent* if you think you qualify for college money. Meet all deadlines for scholarships as well as financial aid. Be careful to use student loans and other money for the necessities of college and not for having a good time while you're there.

Is it worth it to spend $40,000 to $50,000 or more per year to go to a private school? Maybe not, in terms of lifetime earnings. Be sure to investigate state or local colleges, especially if you are strapped for money. The degree is the same whether you live on campus or stay at home with your parents to save money. The experience of living away from home, however, does give you a taste of freedom and responsibility that you don't get if you continue to live at home and go to a nearby college or university.

One tax tip: For your first two years, $2,000 to $4,000 of your college expenses may be tax deductible, depending on your (or your parents') total income. Be sure that you or your parents take advantage of this tax-saving opportunity. After the first two years of postsecondary education, a life-long learning credit of twenty percent is available whenever you pay for classes of *any* kind. Check with an accountant about the tax benefits of education expenses and the limits that change from year to year.

(If you decide to do your taxes yourself, don't waste your money on self-help books at your local bookstore. The IRS puts out a free book, Publication 17, which can be mailed directly to you by calling the IRS.)

Look into education savings plans for your children—and start early. There are many plans, from 529 college accounts to education IRAs. The tax exemption for these plans was made permanent in 2006 (as long as the money is used for education) and some plans may be transferred to another child, in case your brilliant scholar or athlete gets a full ride at the college of his choice! The bottom line is that the cost for your child to attend college may be out of reach unless you plan now.

Another form of higher education is trade schools—sometimes called "career colleges." These schools may prepare you for jobs in areas such as massage therapy, criminal justice, auto technicians, and nurses' assistants. Don't discount these schools. Many of them have smaller classes and better teacher/student ratios than big universities.

Don't just depend on formal education alone. You will continue learning throughout your lifetime. The days of graduating from college or technical school and never having to go back to school or for more training are over. With technology changing as rapidly as it is today, you will spend your life learning and relearning just to keep up with ever-changing trends and technology, some of which will be a part of your chosen career and some of which you will do on your own.

We are constantly being educated through the experiences of daily living, the media, our friends, parents, and in many other ways. Find a "mentor"—someone who is willing to share his knowledge about financial matters with you. Discover a friend who wants to learn as much as you do and exchange ideas and information.

Reading, enrolling in courses of interest, and attending seminars should all be a part of your life-long learning. Read books (***Investment Guide for Teens*** by David and Tom Gardner or ***The Millionaire Next Door*** by Thomas Stanley and William Danko are excellent beginning choices), the financial pages of your newspaper, the Wall Street Journal. Talk to parents, teachers, and other professionals about your goals and plans. Don't be afraid to ask questions—lots of them. Learn from others' mistakes.

Maybe one rationale for parents not talking to their children and teens more about financial matters is that they are embarrassed about the mistakes they have made. We all make lots of financial blunders, but what a valuable learning experience it could be if we would share these with each other!

Pay attention to the average rate of return on the investments you make. The "Rule of 72" means that you divide 72 by your rate of return to figure out how many years it takes to double your investment. Naturally, the higher the rate, the fewer number of years it takes to double your money.

For example, if your interest rate is 6%, 72 divided by 6 equals 12. It would take 12 years to double your money at that rate. But if your rate is 12%, 72 divided by 12 equals 6. You double your investment in 6 years—half the time as the first example.

Remember compounding? It makes a huge difference over a span of twenty to thirty years if you are doubling your money every six years instead of every twelve!

Attend financial seminars to learn more about preparing for your "Financial Independence Day." (The day your money starts working for you instead of you working for your money; in other words, when you're able to live off of your investments.) Learn how to say "No" when bombarded by demands to buy financial products as a result of the seminars you attend. "Free" seminars are just that if you look objectively at the products that are offered and carefully determine what is right for you. There is a wealth of information out there. Locate the financial section at your local library and use it.

Learn what our schools are forgetting to teach.

IMPORTANT INFORMATION

IMPORTANT INFORMATION

_____

_____

_____

_____

_____

_____

_____

_____

_____

_____

_____

_____

_____

_____

_____

_____

_____

_____

_____

GIVE GENEROUSLY, STAY HEALTHY, ENJOY LIFE

"ABUNDANCE IS MEASURED BY HOW MUCH WE SHARE," reads a sign in a little shop in the Arts and Crafts Community of Gatlinburg, Tennessee. Life is not about making and accumulating money for the sake of being wealthy. In the long run, it's not how much you make, but what you do with it and with your life that counts.

As John F. Kennedy said, "Wealth is the means, and people are the ends. All our material riches will avail us little if we do not use them to expand the opportunities of our people." Don't let your financial growth outpace your spiritual and personal growth.

Money gives us choices and enables us to give back to our communities. It allows us to share our money, time, and talents with those around us. One measure of success is how much you give back. Develop a generous and benevolent nature. Giving helps us to be grateful for what we have. Teens are volunteering with their time at a record pace through schools and churches, and that habit will carry through to their adult years. Some high schools are requiring volunteer service as a requirement for graduation, but if yours doesn't, find your own ways to help in your community.

Take pleasure in giving—not only your money, but your time, your experience, your talents and yourself—to your church, your favorite charity, the homeless, the suffering, the less fortunate. Give these gifts, not expecting anything in return. Develop a contributor mentality rather than a consumer mentality. Wear an "apron"—not a "bib."

According to Martha Edelman, President of the Children's Defense Fund, "Service is the rent we pay for living." I believe we are here on earth for a purpose—to *add* to life on earth, not just to *take* from it. The "entitlement" trend in this country (the feeling that the world owes us something—the *"me"* generation) has promoted fiscal irresponsibility. We want instant gratification, no matter what the cost in terms of money or relationships. Generosity is the antidote to excess and self-indulgence. It will transform your life.

This isn't to say you should not be responsible in your giving. Always research organizations before you give them a donation. Andrew Carnegie (for whom Carnegie Hall is named) says, "It is more difficult to give money away intelligently than earn it in the first place."

Investigate what percentage of your money actually goes to starving children in Zimbabwe (or whatever country) and how much goes for administrative expenses or fund raising. Be careful of scams, where your money goes straight into someone's pocket.

Volunteer in your community, your neighborhood, or your church with your time and efforts. Give to the hungry or to underprivileged children. Volunteer to be a "big brother" or a "big sister." It truly is more blessed to give than to receive.

Don't wait until you are "rich" to begin giving, or even until you are out of debt. Establishing an early habit of giving a minimum of ten percent *before* you can really afford to will enable you to give even more generously when you have more to give. Remember, you're already wealthy, compared to the rest of the world. If you have money in the bank, in your pocket, and some change in a dish or jar somewhere, you are in the top *eight percent* of the world's wealth.

Our culture encourages self-centeredness (the *"me"* mentality) even in very young children (think of the Saturday morning cartoons you watched as a child enticing you to buy all sorts of *stuff*). It's all about what *I* want. Parents are hooked on spending, and children get hooked, too. The highest bankruptcy rate ever recorded was in 2002, and bankruptcies among 18- to 25-year-olds keep climbing. This might just be the height of irresponsible fiscal behavior. Most bankruptcies occur because of uncontrolled spending.

We don't always want to take responsibility for our actions—and that includes expecting the government to take care of us if we make irresponsible choices with our money. Many highly paid sports figures and even lottery winners end up broke because they make poor choices. Frivolous lawsuits drain our court system even when it is clear that the person bringing the suit has been irresponsible. Develop a *fiscal* responsibility.

One way to help reach your financial goals is to stay healthy. Lifelong programs of fitness and healthy eating habits go a long way toward protecting your financial future. Choosing a healthy diet and a physical fitness program at an early age (and sticking with it!) goes a long way in launching a lifetime of good health. Those who exercise need assisted living an average of ten to twenty years *later* than whose who don't.

If you are a smoker, *QUIT!* Besides the obvious deadly health risks, by investing the money instead of spending it on your pack-a-day habit, you will build a very sizable nest egg for your future. At a cost of $3.00 per pack, that's $1,095 to put into your millionaire fund *every year.*

Even half a pack per day at a cost of $3.00 per pack is $547 per year. If you invest this money instead, it will bring anywhere from $60,000 to $5 million, not to mention better health and the medical costs you save.

Even with a physical fitness mindset, we have no control over most diseases. Nothing depletes our resources like a debilitating sickness. Use some preventive measures and make sure your insurance coverage is adequate. *Never* be without health insurance. Nothing drains your resources more than a serious illness, injury, or hospital stay without sufficient insurance.

Whether you travel, volunteer in your community, start a business, buy a vacation home to share with friends and family, or help your children and/or grandchildren with education funds, use your financial independence to enjoy yourself and make the world a better place. At whatever age you become independent of earned income, enjoy the wealth from your investments. Be *physically* and *fiscally* fit. It's not what you take with you from this world, but what you leave behind.

"Lives of great men all remind us, we can make our lives sublime.
And departing, leave behind us footprints on the sands of time."
                                                                                    – Henry Wadsworth Longfellow

IMPORTANT INFORMATION

_____

_____

_____

_____

_____

_____

_____

_____

_____

_____

_____

_____

_____

_____

_____

_____

_____

_____

_____

_____

_____

LET YOUR MONEY WORK FOR YOU

HAVING MONEY DOES NOT MAKE YOU A BETTER PER-SON; IT JUST GIVES YOU CHOICES. Proverbs 13:7 in The Living Bible reads, "Some rich people are poor, and some poor people have great wealth." It's not a matter of money, but how you live your life that counts. Saving for your future is not a new concept, either. "The wise man saves for the future, but the foolish man spends whatever he gets" is also in Proverbs (21:20).

There is a difference between living on income and living on wealth. How long do you want to work? Right now, you may feel as though you're indestructible and can work forever. But do you really want to have to work until you're 65, 70, 75?

If your financial goal is to eventually live on your investments and not be forced to work just to buy groceries, start preparing for that time now. Work should be a choice as an older adult, not a necessity. At what point in your life do you want that to happen? The words *elderly* and *poverty* should not materialize in the same breath.

Many things may interfere with the financial goals you set for yourself. One thing is certain, the sooner you start saving for your future, the better your chances of attaining your goals. It doesn't take a lot of money to achieve wealth—a little money and a lot of time work quite well. Remember, how much money you keep and what you do with it is much more important than how much you earn.

The mistake most people say they've made was not getting started earlier. There is never a convenient time to save; there are always many other places to spend your money. The more you make, the more you'll spend. Treat saving and investing as one of your monthly expenses, and *pay yourself first.*

Diversified investments provide better opportunities of reaching your goals than singular investments. Multiple sources of income offer the best chance for financial independence. As you journey thorough your adult life, add different types of investments to your collection. Be on the lookout for opportunities to fund your financial independence. Retirement accounts, mutual funds, and rental property may all be a part of your portfolio. Let these investments work for you instead of your working for them.

Real estate may not be a good choice for young adults because of the cost. Rental property can be lucrative, but it can also be time consuming. You may end up paying a lot for repairs if you can't do them yourself. And you do take the chance of renters damaging your property. But as you get older, you may find that real estate can be a very rewarding part of your portfolio. The value of real estate usually appreciates over the years, adding to your total net worth.

Note: If you are reading this book and you are past your teens and early twenties, it's *never* too late. If you are in your thirties, forties, or fifties, get moving! If you're fifty years old, you have perhaps another

35 years (I know, that's a lifetime to a teen!) Don't put off saving and/or getting out of debt another day longer. Get your financial house in order. **Whatever** you can save is better than having nothing.

Online calculators can help you determine how much you need to save, based on age and current savings. There are many, but here are a few:

- My Plan at Fidelity's web site: http://personalfidelity.com/planning,
- http://jhfunds.com/education/tools.aspx or
- www.Americanfunds.com/retirement/calculator/index.htm?r=t.

Still think you can't afford to put money away for your future? You can't afford *not to!* Make any excuse you want, but you either *will* or *will not* achieve financial independence. It's simply your decision.

The choices you make as a young adult will determine how soon you will reach your goals. You now have no excuse for *not* becoming wealthy. Everyone having the information early enough should retire a millionaire. Saving, investing, and avoiding the pitfalls of credit are all major contributions to financial independence. Look for opportunities to make the most of your current income, and begin now to achieve your own "Financial Independence Day."

Follow these simple steps to begin achieving your financial goals:

1. **GET STARTED!** Start saving money *TODAY.*

2. Make the most of banking and investment opportunities.

3. Open a Roth IRA **now** and a 401(k) when you get a full-time job. Ask your parents or grandparents to help you get started by matching funds that you save.

4. Avoid using credit to buy *stuff* you don't need. Pay off credit cards in full each month. <u>Using credit *always* ties up future income.</u>

5. Build equity in a home. Avoid home equity loans and stay away from car loans for longer than four years.

6. Protect yourself and your loved ones with life and health insurance. Make sure you have renters' insurance when renting an apartment.

7. READ! Ask questions and get educated about financial matters.

8. Give generously (even *before* you can afford it). One-tenth of your income and time is a starting point. Remember, as an American, you're already wealthy compared to the rest of the world.

9. Stay fit and healthy throughout your life with good eating habits and fitness programs.

10. Let *time* make you wealthy. You're on your way to becoming a millionaire!

IMPORTANT INFORMATION

GLOSSARY

401(k): Retirement account available at some companies, sometimes with matching employer funds

Average Rate of Return: The average percentage of interest or growth you earn on your investments over a period of time

Bear Market: When stock prices fall 25% or more

Blue Chip Stock: The most consistently profitable companies

Bonds: Lending corporations or municipalities money on which you will earn interest

Bull Market: Rising stock prices

Certificate of Deposit: A specific amount of money deposited in a bank for a specific time period; usually requires amounts of $1,000 or more

Compounding: Earning interest on the interest you have already earned; the key to successful investing at an early age

Credit: Using future income to buy "stuff" now

Credit Bureaus: Three major companies that keep track of your credit rating

Credit Scores: The number assigned to your personal credit rating used by lenders to determine whether to lend you money, generally ranging from 300 to 850

Debit Card: A card used to withdraw money from an ATM machine or used in a store to pay for a purchase, with payment immediately deducted from your checking account

Depreciation: Decline in value of an asset

Disability Insurance: Protection if you become ill or injured and cannot work for a period of time

Diversification: Spreading out investments to lessen risk

Dollar Cost Averaging: Using a set amount to buy stocks every month whether the price goes up or down

FDIC: Federal Deposit Insurance Corporation, which insures deposits in banks up to $100,000 per account

Inflation: The gradual rise in prices of consumer goods

IRA: Individual Retirement Account set up by individuals; can be a regular IRA or a Roth IRA

Liquidity: How easily your assets can be converted into cash

Mutual Funds: Funds containing 50-100 companies, which can be purchased instead of buying individual stocks and thus spreading out risk

Outstanding checks: The checks you have issued that have not yet been returned to the bank for payment

Payday Lenders: Establishments that will cash a check and hold it for you, charging exorbitant rates of interest to do so

Permanent Life Insurance (Whole Life): Fixed premiums for as long as you live, or until you quit paying on the policy; offers dividends and cash values

Rule of 72: Dividing 72 by your rate of interest to determine how many years it takes to double your investment

Social Security: Government retirement fund that workers pay into during their working years; employers match all contributions

Stock: Ownership in corporations; hopefully earning dividends as well as increasing in value

Tax Deferred: Retirement accounts on which taxes are not paid until withdrawal upon retirement

Term Life Insurance: The cheapest life insurance covering you for a specific time and offering temporary protection

Upside Down Loans: Owing more on an asset than it is worth

IMPORTANT INFORMATION

_____

_____

_____

_____

_____

_____

_____

_____

_____

_____

_____

_____

_____

_____

_____

_____

_____

_____

_____

_____

IMPORTANT INFORMATION

_____

_____

_____

_____

_____

_____

_____

_____

_____

_____

_____

_____

_____

_____

_____

_____

_____

_____